Looking after the sheep wasn't easy work. David had to lead the flock up to the mountain early in the morning, and watch over them while they grazed. Then, in the evening, he had to bring all the sheep safely home again.

David guarded the flock all day, because the mountain was so dangerous. Hungry lions and bears lived there, lying in wait to eat stray sheep. David had to make sure his sheep didn't get eaten, so he watched the flock very carefully. He counted them at lunchtime to make sure none had wandered away, and he checked them again before leading them home. Soon he could recognise every sheep, and had a name for each one.

David was brave and clever, and he made a very good shepherd. He wasn't a bit afraid of the wild animals, although he had only a knife and sling to protect himself. Once or twice a lion did try to steal his sheep, but David chased the lion until he caught up with it. He made it drop the frightened sheep, and then he leapt on to the lion's back and struck it with his knife.

The lion was astonished. It wasn't used to being chased – usually it did the chasing itself! The lions and bears soon learned to keep away from the sheep that David guarded.

Saul, the king of Israel, lived near Bethlehem. One day, when the king was sick, his doctors thought that music would cheer him up and make him feel better. 'Very well then,' grumbled King Saul. 'Find me a harpist and I'll listen to some music.'

One of the king's soldiers had heard David playing his harp, and knew how good he was. When King Saul heard about the shepherd boy he looked up with new interest. That afternoon he decided to send for David.

David's father was astounded, but he dared not argue with the king. He sent one servant to fetch David from the mountain, and another to collect gifts for the king. When David arrived panting, his father was in a dreadful fuss.

'King Saul wants you to play for him, David, so go and wash and then take this bread and wine with you. And perhaps a baby goat as well. Don't forget to brush your hair, and change your tunic too.' David turned to get ready. 'Oh,' called his father, 'and don't forget your harp!'

David played so well that the king felt a lot better. He asked David to stay, and play his harp as often as he could. So David divided his time between serving the king, and looking after his father's sheep.

A few years later the king's army had to get ready for war. An enemy country had challenged King Saul, and brought their troops for battle. The two armies lined up on either side of a big valley, and King Saul prepared to lead his soldiers in the fight.

David was still too young to join the army, and so he had to stay at home and spend all his time with the sheep. But the job he had once enjoyed seemed very boring to him now. He would much rather have been fighting with his soldier brothers for King Saul.

One evening, after David had returned home with the flock, his father saw how sad David looked. 'I know you want to see the army,' he said. 'Why don't you go to the valley tomorrow morning and take some food to your brothers? Give them my love, and tell them to be brave for me, for I am too old to fight.'

David was delighted! He could not fight, but at least he could see what was happening. He bundled up some food, and left as soon as it was light.

When David reached the valley the king's soldiers had left their tents, and were moving into position for battle. David left his bundle with one of the camp guards, and ran off to find his brothers among the soldiers.

But when he found them, he realised that something was very wrong. His brothers were nervous and anxious, and kept glancing across the valley towards the enemy lines. They looked ashamed when David gave them their father's message. King Saul, who stood nearby, looked grim and worried.

'What's the matter?' asked David. 'Why are you all so unhappy? You haven't even started fighting yet!'

His brothers glanced at each other, and then at him. 'Well,' they said at last, 'you're not a soldier, so you really shouldn't know, but we'll tell you as a secret. It's the enemy. They have a terrible weapon we never expected, and we just don't know what to do!'

'A terrible weapon?' exclaimed David. 'What ever do you mean?'

'You'll see in a moment,' answered his brothers. 'Look – there! It's called Goliath!'

Goliath was as tall as a tank, and his bronze armour glittered in the sunlight. He carried a huge spear across his shoulders, and a sword as long as a man in his right hand. Even the soldiers in his own army trembled when they looked at him.

Goliath stepped forward from the enemy ranks. Then he turned to face King Saul's army, and called out to them. His voice carried across the valley like a trumpet blast. David could hear every word.

'Don't bother to line up for battle!' he shouted. 'Just send one man to fight against me. If he wins, we will all be your slaves. But if I win, you will be *our* slaves!'

No one spoke. King Saul's soldiers all turned white when they saw Goliath, and when they heard his message they were horrified. Not one of them was strong enough to fight Goliath alone.

'Ah ha!' roared Goliath. 'Not brave enough, I see. Why don't you all just give up now, you pack of cowards?'

This was too much for David. How dare Goliath be so rude to his people? He turned to King Saul. 'I'll fight the giant,' he said.

At first, King Saul would not let David fight Goliath. 'I know you are brave,' said the king. 'And I know you are a good musician and a fine shepherd. But that man has been a warrior since he was younger than you are now, and he'll kill you!'

But David was sure he could win. 'God looked after me when I fought lions and bears to protect my father's sheep,' he said. 'He'll protect me when I fight for you.' So the king agreed.

'Wear my armour, since you haven't any of your own,' offered King Saul, and he took it off and gave it all to David. But as soon as David tried it on he knew it was impossible. Everything was much too big for him, and he couldn't even walk in it! So he took it off. 'I'll have to fight Goliath in my own way,' he said. Carefully he chose five smooth stones from a stream, took his sling from the pouch on his belt, and walked down into the valley.

Goliath couldn't believe his eyes. They were sending a boy against him! A barefoot boy with no armour, no sword and no shield, just carrying a bit of leather and a few stones. Was it some kind of joke? He smiled scornfully, and strode down into the valley.

'Come on then, little one,' he shouted. 'If you're the best your army can manage, we'll soon be finished. I'll feed you to the bears for breakfast!'

'No you won't,' called David. 'I'm going to do that to *you!*' And he suddenly broke into a run, heading straight for Goliath. The king's soldiers held their breath as they watched, but the enemy soldiers grinned at each other, ready for their triumph.

When David was close enough to Goliath, he paused for a moment. Goliath thought that David had lost his nerve, but he had stopped only to load his sling with one of the stones. Then he ran forward again, whirled the sling, took aim – and let the stone fly. It whistled through the air and struck Goliath in the middle of his forehead. And down crashed the giant to the ground, with a noise that echoed like thunder!

David ran up to the stunned warrior. He took Goliath's sword from his side, and with an enormous effort lifted it into the air. Everyone gasped. The next moment the sword had fallen, and the giant's head was sliced off. David had won!

Cheers rang out from King Saul and his army, as the enemy fell back in dismay. Their great weapon had failed, and they knew there was no hope left. They fled from the valley in panic, chased by the king's soldiers.

David became a hero that day. When the army returned in victory to Bethlehem, people from all over Israel turned out to cheer and congratulate him. Many years later, when King Saul was dead, David became king of Israel himself. He was famous throughout the land, and everyone remembered how, when he was just a shepherd boy, he had killed a giant with a stone.

This story has been told in many different ways for more than three thousand years. It was first written down in a language called Hebrew. Since then, it has been re-told in almost every language used in the world today.

You can find the story of David and Goliath in the Bible. It is in the First Book of Samuel, Chapters 16 and 17.